TAKE THE LEAD

TRUMPET

jazz

In the book	Page no.	On the CD	
		Tuning Tones Track ①	
		Demonstration	**Backing**
Birdland	**3**	Track ②	Track ③
Desafinado	**6**	Track ④	Track ⑤
Don't Get Around Much Anymore	**8**	Track ⑥	Track ⑦
Fascinating Rhythm	**10**	Track ⑧	Track ⑨
Misty	**12**	Track ⑩	Track ⑪
My Funny Valentine	**14**	Track ⑫	Track ⑬
One O'Clock Jump	**16**	Track ⑭	Track ⑮
Summertime	**18**	Track ⑯	Track ⑰

Series Editor: Anna Joyce

Editorial, production and recording: Artemis Music Limited • Design and production: Space DPS Limited • Published 1999

IMP
International
MUSIC
Publications

Birdland

Demonstration

Backing

Music by
Josef Zawinul

Demonstration   Backing

Desafinado

Words by Newton Ferriera de Mendonca
Music by Antonio Carlos Jobim

Moderate Bossa Nova

Don't Get Around Much Anymore

Demonstration   Backing

Music by Duke Ellington

Demonstration

Backing

Fascinating Rhythm

Music and Lyrics by
George Gershwin and Ira Gershwin

Moderate Swing

Misty

Music by Erroll Garner

14

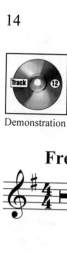

Demonstration   Backing

My Funny Valentine

Music by Richard Rodgers

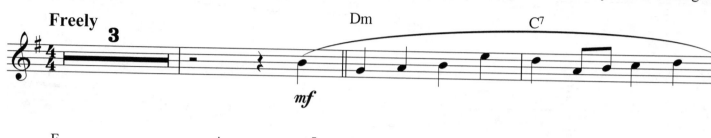

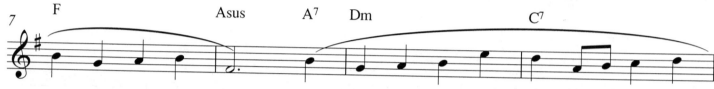

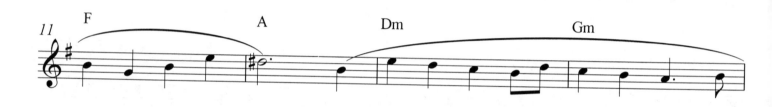

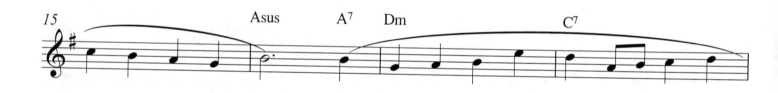

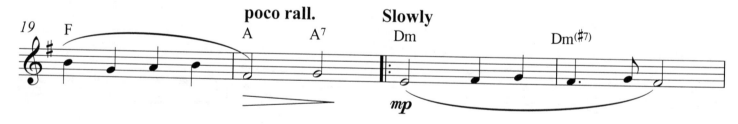

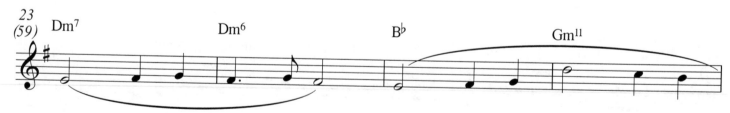

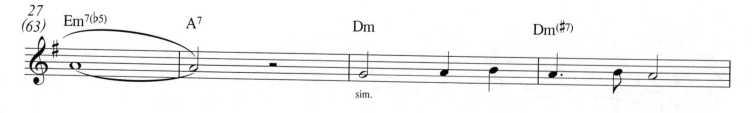

© 1937 & 1999 Chappell & Co Inc, USA
Warner/Chappell Music Ltd, London W6 8BS

Demonstration

Backing

One O'Clock Jump

Music by Count Basie

Bright Swing

Summertime

Demonstration   Backing

Music and Lyrics by George Gershwin,
Du Bose and Dorothy Heyward and Ira Gershwin

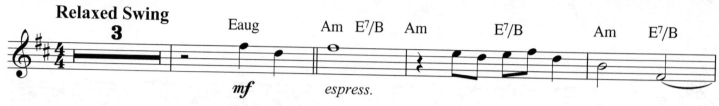

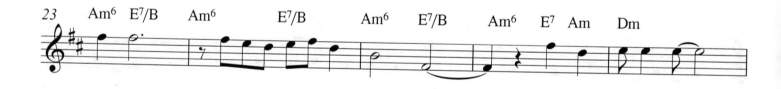

Reproduced and printed by
Halstan & Co. Ltd., Amersham, Bucks., England

You can be the featured soloist with
TAKE THE LEAD

Collect these titles, each with demonstration and full backing tracks on CD.

90s Hits

The Air That I Breathe
(Simply Red)

Angels
(Robbie Williams)

How Do I Live
(LeAnn Rimes)

I Don't Want To Miss A Thing
(Aerosmith)

I'll Be There For You
(The Rembrandts)

My Heart Will Go On
(Celine Dion)

**Something About The Way
You Look Tonight**
(Elton John)

Frozen
(Madonna)

Order ref: 6725A – Flute

Order ref: 6726A – Clarinet

Order ref: 6727A – Alto Saxophone

Order ref: 6728A – Violin

Movie Hits

Because You Loved Me
(Up Close And Personal)

Blue Monday
(The Wedding Singer)

**(Everything I Do)
I Do It For You**
(Robin Hood: Prince Of Thieves)

I Don't Want To Miss A Thing
(Armageddon)

I Will Always Love You
(The Bodyguard)

Star Wars (Main Title)
(Star Wars)

The Wind Beneath My Wings
(Beaches)

You Can Leave Your Hat On
(The Full Monty)

Order ref: 6908A – Flute

Order ref: 6909A – Clarinet

Order ref: 6910A – Alto Saxophone

Order ref: 6911A –Tenor Saxophone

Order ref: 6912A – Violin

TV Themes

Coronation Street

**I'll Be There For You
(theme from Friends)**

Match Of The Day

(Meet) The Flintstones

Men Behaving Badly

Peak Practice

The Simpsons

The X-Files

Order ref: 7003A – Flute

Order ref: 7004A – Clarinet

Order ref: 7005A – Alto Saxophone

Order ref: 7006A – Violin

Christmas Songs

**The Christmas Song
(Chestnuts Roasting On An
Open Fire)**

Frosty The Snowman

**Have Yourself A Merry
Little Christmas**

Little Donkey

**Rudolph The Red-Nosed
Reindeer**

**Santa Claus Is Comin'
To Town**

Sleigh Ride

Winter Wonderland

Order ref: 7022A – Flute

Order ref: 7023A – Clarinet

Order ref: 7024A – Alto Saxophone

Order ref: 7025A – Violin

Order ref: 7026A – Piano

Order ref: 7027A – Drums

The Blues Brothe

**She Caught The Katy And
Left Me A Mule To Ride**

Gimme Some Lovin'

Shake A Tail Feather

**Everybody Needs Somebo
To Love**

The Old Landmark

Think

Minnie The Moocher

Sweet Home Chicago

Order ref: 7079A - Flute

Order ref: 7080A - Clarinet

Order ref: 7081A - Alto Saxophon

Order ref: 7082A - Tenor Saxopho

Order ref: 7083A - Trumpet

Order ref: 7084A - Violin